THE SMART KID'S GUIDE TO
Losing a Pet

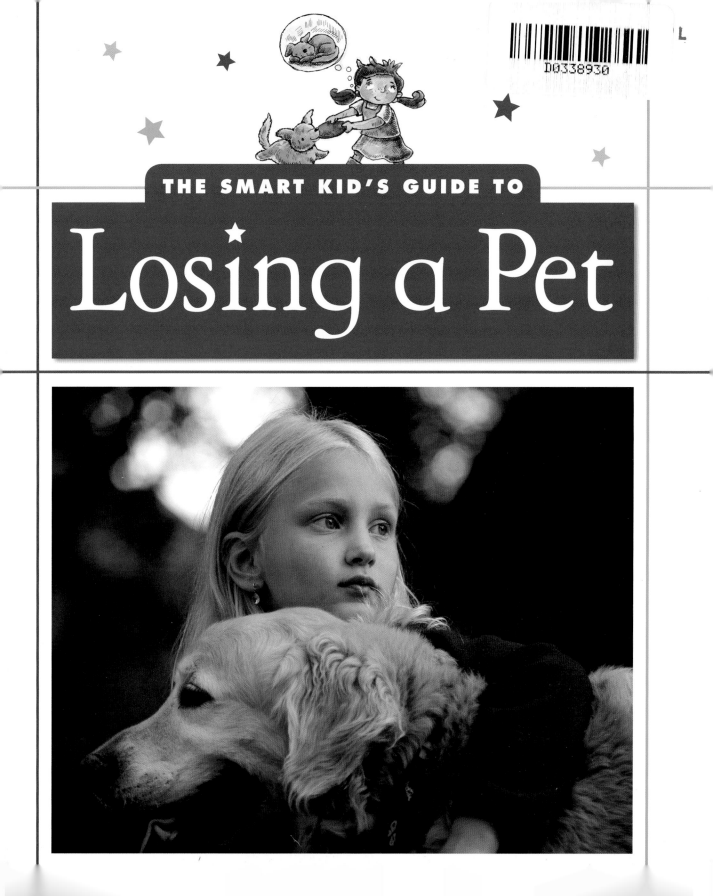

The Child's World

Published by The Child's World®
1980 Lookout Drive • Mankato, MN 56003-1705
800-599-READ • www.childsworld.com

Acknowledgments
The Child's World®: Mary Berendes, Publishing Director
Content Adviser: Philip C. Rodkin, Professor of Child
Development, Departments of Educational Psychology and
Psychology, University of Illinois
The Design Lab: Design
Red Line Editorial: Editorial Direction
Amnet: Production

Photographs ©: iStockphoto/Thinkstock, cover, 1, 26; Nate
Allred/Shutterstock Images, 6; Shutterstock Images, 7, 8, 9,
11, 12, 15, 16, 19, 21, 25; Channarong Meesuk/Shutterstock
Images, 14; Gladskikh Tatiana/Shutterstock Images, 17; Liz Van
Steenburgh/Shutterstock Images, 20; Fer Gregory/Shutterstock
Images, 23; Edward Fielding/Shutterstock Images, 28

ISBN 9781626873469
LCCN 2014930683

Printed in the United States of America
Mankato, MN
July, 2014
PA02224

ABOUT THE AUTHOR

Before becoming a freelance writer, Christine Petersen enjoyed diverse careers as a biologist and middle school science teacher. She has published more than 50 books for young people, covering topics in science, social studies, and health. Christine is a member of the Society of Children's Book Writers and Illustrators.

ABOUT THE ILLUSTRATOR

Ronnie Rooney took art classes constantly as a child. She was always drawing and painting at her mom's kitchen table. She got her BFA in painting from the University of Massachusetts at Amherst and her MFA in illustration from the Savannah College of Art and Design in Savannah, Georgia. Ronnie lives on a U.S. Army base with her infantryman husband and two small children. Ronnie hopes to pass on her love of art and sports to her kids.

CONTENTS

CHAPTER 1

Part of the Family

Do you have a pet? Or have you had one in the past? What was it like when you first met your pet? For some people, that is a magical moment. It feels like you belong together. Or maybe you took some time to get to know your pet. The friendship grew slowly. Or maybe your family had your pet already when you were born. It does not matter how your story started. Once a pet becomes your friend, it is in your heart forever.

Animals and people have not always lived together. Scientists use fossils to understand how those friendships began. Fossils are the hardened remains of things that lived long ago. They show that wolves were the first wild animals to be **tamed** and live near people. This happened in Europe at least 32,000 years ago. People at that time moved from place to place. They hunted meat and gathered plants for food. Wolves might have followed the hunters searching for leftover meat. The two **species** slowly learned to work together. People provided food. Wolves protected them in return. In time, tame wolves became different than their wild cousins. They were faithful to people. They were dogs.

Cats were wild until about 12,000 years ago. Things changed when people began to settle down

Pets can come in many shapes, sizes, and types.

on farms and in towns. The first villages were located in a region called the Near East. This region now includes the countries of Turkey, Syria, and Iraq. Those ancient people learned to grow wheat and other grains that could be made into bread. Mice found and ate some of the grain. Wild cats came into villages to hunt the mice. Like dogs, cats slowly learned to live among people.

Today, more than 164 million Americans live with cats and dogs. We have many other kinds of pets, too. Some are bigger than you! Others are small enough to fit in your pocket. Your pet might be a small and furry hamster, mouse, or guinea pig. It could be an animal with feathers, fins, scales, or even a shell.

Have you ever had a pet you loved?

Many families have pets that they love.

Pets are around when you need them. They are fun to play with. They are often interesting to watch. Pets keep you company when you are lonely. And they are good listeners whenever you need to talk. Pets are different from people in many ways. But they are part of the family, and we usually love them. That is why you feel so sad when a pet dies. It is painful to lose someone you love.

Do you have a favorite photo of your pet? If not, you can draw one. Make a frame for the picture with cardboard or craft sticks. Your framed picture is a special way to keep your friend close by. It can remind you of the great times you spent together.

CHAPTER 2
Part of Life

You may have learned about the life **cycle** in school. A cycle is a set of events that happen over and over again. In the life cycle, there are stages called birth, growth, and change. For example, caterpillars hatch

Life can become more difficult for a pet as it ages.

from eggs. They grow and then become butterflies or moths. Kittens are born from their mothers, not from eggs. A kitten does not look much different than its parent. But it grows bigger and changes by learning new skills.

Death is the other important stage of any life cycle. Death is when life comes to an end.

The veterinarian will help your pet stay as healthy as possible through its life.

All living things will die someday. A pet that lives a long life will die of old age. Its body slows down and weakens over time. Older pets sometimes die of a heart attack or stroke. But death is not always so quick. Your older pet might not be able to eat enough. Its eyesight may be so poor that it cannot walk.

Veterinarians help pets stay healthy and live longer. But they cannot change how the life cycle works. If your pet is old or very sick, the veterinarian might not be able to help it get well. Your pet might be in pain or unable to eat or move around. Sometimes the veterinarian can only help by giving a special shot. Your pet dies right afterward. It feels no fear. The shot does not hurt. This is called **euthanasia**. It is very hard for a family to make this decision. But it can also be the most caring choice for a dear pet. Your family can choose to be with your pet when it dies. Or you can say good-bye and tell your pet that you love it.

No one expects a younger pet to die. But this happens, too. Pets of any age can become seriously ill. Or they might be wounded in an accident. It is hard that we never know when or how a pet will die.

Some families bury their pets after they die.

You might want to see your pet after it dies. Or you might want to remember how it was when alive. Either choice is okay. Your family will decide how to take care of its body. Sometimes people like to bury a pet in the yard. Parents can find out if your city allows this. What if you don't have a yard? Many towns also have a pet **cemetery**. When a pet is buried, its body is usually put in a box. The box goes into the ground and is covered with dirt. You can plant grass or flowers over it. Or your family might choose **cremation**. People have also used this method for thousands of years. The body is burned in a hot fire. Your family can decide to keep the ashes that are left behind. Some people bury the ashes or keep them in a special box at home.

A container with ashes can be part of a memorial to your pet.

Have you ever felt grief? How did you feel?
What did you do to feel better?

Death is confusing. Someone we love is there, and then he or she is gone. **Grief** is the great sadness that comes with losing something or someone you love.

It is hard because we cannot control grief. The feelings come up in different ways and at unexpected times. Everyone goes through grief differently. Some people are quiet and want to be alone with their feelings. Others need to talk, cry, laugh, or yell. The only cure for grief is to let it out.

Death is not like sleep. Your pet will not wake up again. But you do not have to forget your friend. Write a story about a special time you spent together. You can even make a whole book full of stories! Share your book with friends and family members. Maybe they will also have favorite stories to add.

 Saying Good-Bye

You will probably have a lot of questions after your pet's death. But it can be hard to know how to ask about such big topics. Adults are sometimes afraid to bring it up, too. They don't want to upset you. Here are some common questions that people think about and talk about.

What happens after death? No one knows what happens when a person or pet dies. Death is a mystery.

But everyone has ideas. For example, ancient Egyptians believed in life after death. Cats were often **mummified** after they died. One cemetery in Egypt contains more than 300,000 cat mummies! Mummified bodies do not decay. The Egyptians protected the body so the spirit could move on to the afterlife. They hoped the cat would live with its family forever.

Some people believe that the dead go to heaven. People and pets all meet there after death. Other people believe that the soul is born into a new body. Some people believe that death can be seen simply as an ending. Talk to your parents. They can share their thoughts and beliefs about death. You can share your thoughts and beliefs, too.

Cats were important in the ancient Egyptian religion.

You can't stop every accident from happening.

Was it my fault? **Guilt** can come up when you are grieving. It is an achy feeling that maybe you did something wrong. Children and even adults worry and wonder if they might have caused a pet's death. Perhaps they didn't lock a gate and the pet ran out. Or they forgot to feed the pet once. Sometimes we get mad at our pets. We wish they would go just away. If the pet dies afterward, you might feel **responsible**. Do not blame yourself. Your wishes cannot cause bad things to happen. And sometimes accidents happen even when people are very careful. Pets die because they grow old, become sick, or have accidents.

If your pet is lost or dies, it sometimes helps to remember the good times you had together.

Will I always feel so bad? Grief is a mishmash of feelings. It may show up one day as sadness. That is because you miss your pet so much. The next day, you might feel great joy that you had such a good friend at all. People sometimes feel mad after a death, too. They are hurt about being left alone. Or maybe they believe someone caused their pet's death. When you keep bad feelings inside, they hurt even more.

Remember that grief is more than a bunch of feelings. It is also a **process**. You can get through it step by step. One important step is to let your feelings out by sharing them with someone you trust. Do not hide them. Cry if you feel the need. Laugh when something is funny. It is not wrong to feel happy while you are grieving. Talk with other people who loved your pet. Is that too hard? Try writing in a journal instead. You don't need to buy anything fancy. Just take out a blank school notebook or fold together a few sheets of blank paper. There is no right or wrong way to keep a journal. It can hold a list of words that describe your feelings. Or maybe you would like to write letters to your pet.

You will not forget your animal friend. But you will begin to remember your pet with a smile instead of tears.

Some pets run away or become lost. You can put up "lost pet" signs with a picture and phone number. A person might call if they find your pet. Sadly, some pets never make it home. This feels like a death, even though you don't know for sure what happened. Let yourself grieve and remember your pet with love.

CHAPTER 4

Good Memories

There are many ways to honor and remember your pet. At first you might not like this idea. You might think it is easier just to be alone. But try taking the risk. Most people find that it feels good to celebrate the life of someone they love. Sharing good memories can help you through the grieving process.

You can plan a **funeral** or other service after your pet's death. Invite family, friends, and neighbors who cared about him. Funerals are not really for the dead. They are a way for the living to say good-bye. The service does not have to be sad or serious. You can play music, sing, or read a poem. Sharing memories with others is an important step in letting go of your grief.

Consider holding a funeral for your pet.

A memorial can be anything that helps you remember your pet.

Have you ever seen a **memorial**? It is a lasting reminder of someone who died. You can choose to make almost any kind of memorial for your pet. Maybe you would like to put a stone on the spot where your pet is buried. Did your pet love to sleep in a sunny corner of the house? You could put a little statue in that spot. Or you might plant a tree in the park where it liked to run and play. Other members of your family might also want to make a memorial for your pet. Each of you remembers your pet differently.

Photos capture our memories forever. When you are ready, look through photos showing your pet's life. Sit down and look through them with your family. You can share special stories of your pet. You might cry a little. You will probably laugh a lot. All your feelings are okay! Have your favorite photos printed and paste them into a book. Then you will always be able to find them. You can write stories in the book. Or add special items that tell about your pet's life. Even the corner of a food bag has meaning if it reminds you of the time you spent together.

Eventually, you may want a new pet to love.

Grief can be slow. You must be patient to let your heart heal. But don't worry. There will come a time when you do not look for your pet around every corner. The memories of him will not sting anymore. Instead, they will be sweet and comforting. Then you might want to welcome a new animal friend into the house. Have a family meeting to talk about it. Does everyone feel ready? You have a lot of love to give. A pet will be lucky to share it.

Your parents or other adult family members may have lost a pet before. Ask how they met that pet. What happened to cause its death? And how did the adult deal with his or her feelings of grief? Sharing stories can bring you closer. Sharing helps you know that you are not alone. You might even learn something about how to heal.

TOP TEN THINGS TO KNOW

1. Death is a natural part of the life cycle.
2. Take your pet to see a veterinarian if she is ill or sick. A healthy pet lives longer.
3. You should not blame yourself for a pet's death.
4. Let out your grief by talking, writing, crying— whatever feels right to you. Everyone grieves in different ways.
5. Try not to spend too much time alone with your grief. Family and friends can help you feel better.
6. A funeral or other ceremony can help you celebrate your pet after her death.
7. Make a memorial as a lasting reminder of your pet's life.
8. Sharing stories is another special way of remembering your pet.
9. You will love your pet forever.
10. It is okay to make room in your heart for another pet someday.

GLOSSARY

cemetery (SEM-i-ter-ee) A cemetery is a place where the dead are buried. Some communities have a cemetery just for pets.

cremation (kree-MAY-shun) Cremation is the burning of a dead body. After a cremation, the family can keep their pet's ashes.

cycle (SYE-kuhl) A cycle is a set of events that happen over and over. The life cycle includes birth, growth, change, and death.

euthanasia (yoo-thuh-NAY-zhuh) Euthanasia is helping an animal die without pain. Some families choose euthanasia if their pet is very sick.

funeral (FYOO-nur-uhl) A funeral is a service to remember someone who died. You can invite your friends and family to a funeral for your pet.

grief (GREEF) Grief is a feeling of deep sorrow. People feel grief when someone dies.

guilt (GILT) Guilt is a feeling that you did something wrong. You might feel guilt if you forget to feed your pet.

memorial (muh-MOR-ee-uhl) A memorial is a lasting reminder of someone who died. You can build a memorial to help you remember your pet.

mummified (MUHM-uh-fyed) Something that is mummified has been wrapped up so it will not decay. Ancient Egyptians mummified humans and animals after they died.

process (PRAH-ses) A process is something that happens step by step. Grieving is a process.

responsible (ri-SPAHN-suh-buhl) Someone who is responsible is in charge of something or to blame for it happening. Some people feel they are responsible after their pet dies.

species (SPEE-sheez) Species are different kinds of living things. Dogs, wolves, and people are all different species.

tamed (TAYMD) Something that is tamed is no longer wild. Early humans tamed wild wolves.

veterinarians (vet-ur-uh-NAIR-ee-uhns) Veterinarians are animal doctors. Veterinarians can help a sick pet get well.

BOOKS

Mansfield, Monica. *When You Have to Say Goodbye: Loving and Letting Go of Your Pet*. Midway, FL: Beanpole Books, 2011.

Wilson, Wayne L. *Kate, the Ghost Dog: Coping with the Death of a Pet*. Washington, DC: Magination Press, 2010.

WEB SITES

Visit our Web site for links about losing a pet:
childsworld.com/links

Note to Parents, Teachers, and Librarians:
We routinely verify our Web links to make sure they are safe and active sites. So encourage your readers to check them out!

INDEX